Fact Finders®

PERSPECTIVES on HISTORY

CHRISTOPHER COLUMBUS

NEW WORLD EXPLORER OR FORTUNE HUNTER?

by Jessica Gunderson

Consultant:
William D. Phillips, Jr.
Professor of History
University of Minnesota

CAPSTONE PRESS
a capstone imprint

Fact Finders Books are published by Capstone Press,
1710 Roe Crest Drive, North Mankato, Minnesota 56003
www.capstonepub.com

Library of Congress Cataloging-in-Publication Data
Gunderson, Jessica.
Christopher Columbus : new world explorer or fortune hunter? / by Jessica Gunderson.
pages cm. — (Fact finders. Perspectives on history)
Includes bibliographical references and index.
Summary: "Explores the life of Christopher Columbus through his exploration of the New
World"—Provided by publisher.
ISBN 978-1-4765-0242-7 (library binding)
ISBN 978-1-4765-3406-0 (paperback)
ISBN 978-1-4765-3414-5 (ebook PDF)
1. Columbus, Christopher—Juvenile literature. 2. Explorers—America—Biography—Juvenile
literature. 3. Explorers—Spain—Biography—Juvenile literature. 4. America—Discovery and
exploration—Spanish—Juvenile literature. I. Title.
E111.G86 2014
970.01'5092—dc23
[B]   2013007329

Editorial Credits
Abby Colich, editor; Ted Williams, designer; Svetlana Zhurkin, media researcher;
Laura Manthe, production specialist

Photo Credits
Alamy: Hilary Morgan, 21, Walker Art Library, 6; Architect of the Capitol, cover (detail, bottom
left), 12; Bridgeman Art Library: Look and Learn/Private Collection, 18; Corbis: Bettmann, 22;
Library of Congress, cover (middle right), 9, 11, 14, 25, 27; Newscom: Prisma/Kurwenal/Album,
5; North Wind Picture Archives, 17; Shutterstock: Alena Hovorkova (design elements), throughout,
Dianka Pyzhova (design elements), throughout, exshutter (vintage paper sheet), throughout,
Mesut Dogan, 28, Oleksiy Fedorov (background texture), throughout, Triff, cover (background)

Direct Quotes
p. 13 from *Journals and Other Documents on the Life and Voyages of Christopher Columbus*, translated
and edited by Samuel Eliot Morison (New York: Limited Editions Club, 1963), pp. 122–123.
p. 17 from Morison, p. 245.
p. 19 from *Columbus: The Four Voyages* by Laurence Bergreen (New York: Viking, 2011), p. 207.

Printed in the United States of America in Brainerd, Minnesota.
032013   007721BANGF13

TABLE OF CONTENTS

Who Was Christopher Columbus?

Christopher Columbus was a brave, bold, and brilliant sailor. He also longed for power and wealth. Many see him as a hero who discovered the Americas. His voyages opened the door for European settlement in the New World. Others view him as a villain who destroyed native peoples and their cultures. Which perspective is true?

WHO DISCOVERED AMERICA?

Was Columbus really the first to discover the Americas? Although he is given the most credit, others had sailed the waters before him. In the 900s, Norse Vikings reached present-day Canada. But they only settled there for a short time. Some have said that Chinese or African sailors first landed in the Americas. But there is no proof of this. Also, about 20,000 years ago, people began to move to North America from Asia. Over many years, they spread throughout the Americas. They created their own cultures and civilizations. Therefore, Columbus did not actually "discover" an unpopulated land.

Christopher Columbus was an expert sailor.

settlement: a group of people living in a new village or area

New World: a name for North and South America

civilization: a society that is highly developed

Chapter 1

SAILING DREAMS

Christopher Columbus was born in 1451 in Genoa, Italy. For several years he sailed as a businessman on **merchant** ships. During his travels he observed the ocean, the winds, the current, and the stars. Columbus eventually settled in Portugal. But he never lost the desire to explore.

Even as a young man, Columbus was interested in sailing.

FACT

Columbus' son wrote that when pirates attacked Columbus' merchant ship in 1476, he jumped overboard. He used an oar to swim 6 miles (9.7 kilometers) to shore.

In the 1400s silk, jewels, and spices from Asia were popular in Europe. Merchants traveled across Asia on land to trade for these goods. But in 1453 the Ottoman Turks captured Constantinople, the center of trade. This takeover made trade with Asia more difficult for Europeans.

European explorers searched for another route to Asia. They sailed down the coast of Africa, looking for a passage east. When Columbus heard of these explorations, an idea blazed in his mind. What if instead of sailing south, he sailed west?

SAILING THE OCEAN SEA

Some legends say people told Columbus his journey would fail because Earth is flat. However, in the 1400s, most educated Europeans knew that Earth was round. But they did believe Earth contained only one large area of land. This land was surrounded by a giant body of water called the Ocean Sea.

merchant: a person who buys and sells goods for profit

Columbus knew another trade route to Asia would bring large profits to European merchants. If he were the first to discover a new route, he could become rich too. Columbus had heard there was gold in Asia. Europeans needed gold for trade.

To carry out his plan, Columbus needed money. He brought his idea to the Portuguese king. But the king turned him down. In 1486 Columbus traveled to Spain. He told King Ferdinand and Queen Isabella about his plan.

Queen Isabella listened closely. Columbus promised wealth and glory for Spain. Isabella set up a committee to consider Columbus' ideas.

The committee questioned Columbus' plan. The world was too large, they said. Columbus would never be able to return from such a long journey. And Columbus had too many demands. He insisted that he be named admiral of the Ocean Sea and royal governor of any new lands. He also wanted 10 percent of all profits.

profit: money that a business makes

committee: a group of people chosen to discuss things and make decisions for a larger group

admiral: an officer with a high rank

The royal committee had long, heated discussions about whether or not to fund Columbus' trip.

For six years Columbus waited. He was confident that he would find a westward route to Asia. Finally, in 1492 Isabella agreed to fund Columbus' journey.

FACT

The grand total for Columbus' seven months of sea exploration cost about 1,765,734 Spanish maravedis. That amount is equal to $294,000 in today's money.

Chapter 2

JOURNEY TO THE UNKNOWN

Columbus, along with about 90 sailors, left Spain on August 2, 1492. Columbus was captain of the lead ship, the *Santa Maria*. Two other ships, the *Niña* and the *Pinta*, followed.

Columbus relied upon his knowledge of the sea to guide him. He paid close attention to tides, winds, the color of the sea, and the clouds. He tracked the ships' location. To judge the ships' speed, he noted how long it took to pass an object, such as floating driftwood. By keeping track of the speed and the hours sailed, he was able to judge the distance traveled.

As the days went on, the crew became upset. They hadn't seen land for weeks. They became worried they were too far from home and would never return. On October 10 some sailors planned to throw Columbus overboard.

Columbus was aware of the men's unease. The ships had spent more than two months at sea. Columbus promised that if they didn't spot land within three days, he'd consider returning. Two days later they finally spotted land.

The crew was overwhelmed when land was finally spotted.

FACT

Queen Isabella promised a reward for the first sailor to spot land. On October 12 a lookout named Rodrigo de Triana spotted land and shouted for joy. But Columbus claimed the queen's reward for himself, stating that he'd seen a flickering light the night before.

Columubs said the land he found belonged to Spain, even though people already lived there.

At dawn on October 12, the three ships reached an island. Columbus believed it to be in the East Indies, islands off the coast of Asia. Raising the Spanish flag, Columbus claimed the island for Spain, naming it San Salvador.

Columbus was actually in the present-day Bahamas. There he encountered several Tainos, the native islanders. He called them "Indians," thinking he was in the Indies. The Tainos were a peaceful people. They lived in huts and grew vegetables. They also caught fish to eat. The Tainos were friendly to the newcomers. They were willing to trade items such as parrots, cloth, and pottery. Columbus was curious about the Tainos. However, he thought they could be easily conquered.

The Tainos had very little gold, disappointing Columbus. They told him of lands to the north that had gold and pearls. Columbus set off to find the treasures.

COLUMBUS' JOURNAL ENTRY, DECEMBER 16, 1492

"They [The Tainos] bear no arms, and are completely defenseless and of no skill in arms, and very cowardly, so that a thousand would not face three; and so they are fit to be ordered about and made to work, to sow and do all else that may be needed."

Queen Isabella and King Ferdinand listened to tales of Columbus' travels.

14

For two months Columbus explored nearby islands, including present-day Hispaniola and Cuba. He was looking for gold and mainland Asia. Many of the natives he encountered wore gold jewelry. He asked where gold could be found. The natives told him gold was either to the north or inland.

In late December Columbus decided to return to Europe to report to the king and queen. Although he had no gold, he loaded the ships with several Tainos, plants, and animals. He wanted to prove he'd made it across the world.

On December 24 the *Santa Maria* hit shallow, rocky waters and began to sink. The crew saved whatever they could. But the *Santa Maria* was wrecked. The *Niña* and the *Pinta* did not have enough room to carry all the sailors back to Europe. Columbus used the wreckage to build a fort on Hispaniola. He named it La Navidad. Several men would live there until Columbus could return.

In mid-March 1493, Columbus arrived in Spain. He told tales of paradise and jewels, a land full of gold and pearls. He also stated that Cuba was much larger than it actually was. The royal court showered him with attention and celebrations. As his stories spread throughout Spain, Columbus achieved the fame he'd always desired.

Chapter 3

THE LURE OF GOLD

Columbus promised the queen that there was gold on the islands. He suggested starting Spanish colonies there. He thought little about the natives already living on the islands. To him, they were a lesser people.

Queen Isabella quickly gave money for a second trip to colonize the islands. She named Columbus governor of the new lands. Sailors rushed to join Columbus, drawn by the idea of paradise and gold.

In September 1493 Columbus left with 17 ships and about 1,200 men. His brothers Diego and Bartholomew were a part of the crew. Columbus and his men arrived at La Navidad in November. But they found the settlement in ashes and everyone dead. The Tainos told Columbus that the Spaniards had mistreated the natives and the natives fought back.

All 39 men Columbus left behind at La Navidad were killed in the fight with natives.

RESPECT FOR COLUMBUS

"Great praise is due to Admiral Columbus, who first in our era conducted a fleet into the Indian Ocean."
—Guillermo Coma, a settler who came with Columbus on his second voyage, 1493

colony: a place that is settled by people from another country and is controlled by that country

colonize: to settle and control a territory outside of one's own country

Columbus and the Europeans built a new settlement on Hispaniola. They called it Isabela. The new settlers had heard Columbus' stories and expected paradise. However, all they found was hard work—building in the heat, planting crops, and hours of panning for gold. Columbus forced the settlers to keep working.

Natives suffered even more at the hands of Columbus. He demanded that each Taino over the age of 14 find a certain amount of gold. If they didn't, they would have a hand chopped off.

DISAPPROVAL OF COLUMBUS

"The Admiral [Columbus] ... ordered [the settlers] to work hungry, weak, and some sick ... they were all anguished and afflicted and desperate."—Juan de Aguado, a Spaniard sent by the king and queen to the settlement, 1495

Columbus saw another way to make a profit—the slave trade. He ordered his men to capture thousands of natives and send them to Europe as slaves. Columbus also told the settlers to enslave as many natives as they wished. The colonists stormed native villages, burned huts to the ground, and captured the natives. The natives tried to fight back against the Europeans. But their bows and clubs stood no chance against the Europeans' swords and armor. Thousands of natives killed themselves to avoid becoming slaves.

FACT

When 500 enslaved natives arrived in Spain, Queen Isabella was horrified. She wanted no part of the slave trade. She sent the natives back to Hispaniola.

Spaniards destroyed native villages and took the people as slaves.

Chapter 4

TROUBLE IN THE COLONIES

In 1496 Columbus placed his brothers, Bartholomew and Diego, in charge of Hispaniola. Columbus then returned to Spain for the second time. But he did not receive glory and honor. Word of Columbus' treatment of the natives and hard life for settlers had reached many in Spain. A year and a half later, the king and queen finally allowed Columbus a third journey.

Columbus chose not to deal with the upset settlers on Hispaniola. He sent supply ships to the island and continued sailing around the area instead. His goal was still to find a route to Asia. He explored present-day Venezuela and its large rivers. For the first time, Columbus began to suspect he'd found a new continent instead of Asia.

On his third voyage, Columbus sailed around the Gulf of Paria, between present-day Trinidad and Venezuela.

FACT

Columbus had trouble finding sailors for his third voyage. So Isabella agreed to free prisoners if they sailed with him. Columbus ended up with 10 murderers on his ships.

Columbus in chains

In August 1498 Columbus returned to Hispaniola. He found half of the colonists at war against his brothers. Francisco Roldán, a settler left in charge of Isabela, had organized a **rebellion**. He wanted to set up a separate settlement. Columbus tried to make peace with the settlers. He promised them either their own land or a safe return to Spain. When some settlers refused to give in, Columbus ordered several of them hanged.

Meanwhile, Francisco de Bobadilla came to check on Columbus' governing. He was an agent sent by the king and queen. When Bobadilla arrived, he was shocked to see Spaniards hanging from the **gallows**. He immediately stripped Columbus of his power. He also took Columbus' money and gold. In 1500 Bobadilla sent Columbus back to Spain in chains.

Some settlers returned to Spain to tell of Columbus' terrible control of the colony. The king and queen were very upset. They took away his titles of admiral and governor. But they let him keep his earnings and did not charge him with any crimes.

rebellion: a fight against the people in charge
gallows: a wooden frame that holds a rope used to hang criminals

Columbus lived in Spain for a while but was not happy. He still had not fulfilled his dream to discover a new route to Asia. He convinced the king and queen to fund a fourth trip. However, they did not allow him to return to Hispaniola.

With four ships Columbus set sail in 1502. In 1503 Columbus shipwrecked on the island of present-day Jamaica. He sent a few of his men on canoes to Hispaniola, about 100 miles (161 km) away, to beg for help. The new governor of Hispaniola reluctantly agreed. But the rescue crew did not arrive for seven months.

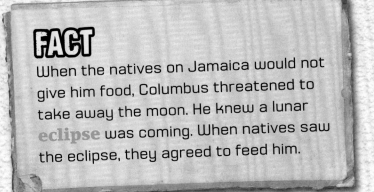

FACT

When the natives on Jamaica would not give him food, Columbus threatened to take away the moon. He knew a lunar **eclipse** was coming. When natives saw the eclipse, they agreed to feed him.

eclipse: an astronomical event in which the earth's shadow passes over the moon or the moon's shadow passes over the earth

Knowing he was unwelcome in Hispaniola, Columbus returned to Spain in 1504. He was wealthy from his profits. But he still believed the Spanish crown owed him more. Queen Isabella was dead. Columbus asked King Ferdinand to make him governor of Hispaniola once again. He asked for more profits too. Even though the New World colonies were becoming successful, Ferdinand refused.

Columbus spent his remaining years writing about his explorations, often with help from his sons Diego and Ferdinand. Columbus died on May 20, 1506.

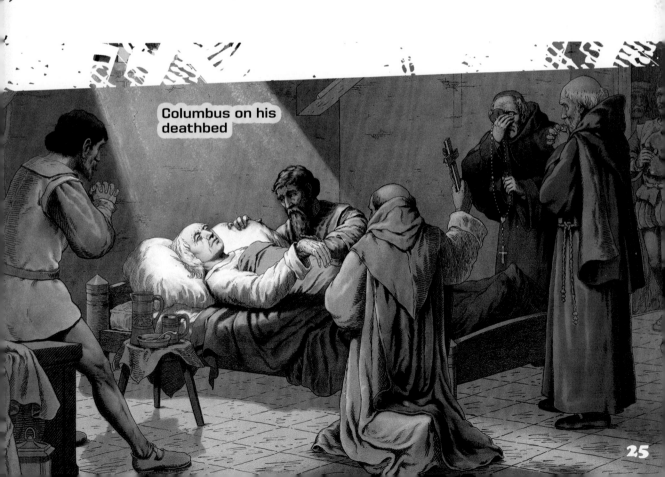

Columbus on his deathbed

Chapter 5

COLUMBUS' LEGACY

Columbus' obsession with finding a new route to Asia opened up a new world for Europeans. Gold and silver were discovered in the Americas in the early 1500s. Settlers traded these precious metals as well as sugar and tobacco. Trade became a major source of wealth for settlers.

Spain continued to settle much of the New World. It became the most powerful nation in the world in the 1500s and 1600s. Today North and South America are made up of 35 countries. Most of them are Spanish-speaking.

Columbus was all but forgotten in the years after his death. It wasn't until centuries later that he was hailed as a hero. American colonists during the **Revolutionary War** (1775–1783) spread the idea that Columbus discovered the New World. Biographers and historians celebrated his voyages. Cities and streets were named after him. In 1937 Columbus Day became a U.S. holiday.

This statue of Christopher Columbus in Philadelphia was built in 1876.

Revolutionary War: the American Colonies' fight for freedom from Great Britain

Over time these views changed. Many began to see Columbus as a villain whose discoveries led to the end of the native way of life. Settlers brought in diseases that wiped out entire communities. War destroyed whole societies. The settlers enslaved, killed, and stole from native peoples. Before Columbus arrived, at least 300,000 Tainos lived in Hispaniola. By 1542 only 500 remained. More than 90 percent died due to slavery, famine, war, and diseases.

A statue of a crouching American Indian at the Christopher Columbus monument in Washington, D.C. honors the natives who died.

In the late 1900s, some people started celebrating **Indigenous** Peoples Day instead of Columbus Day. American Indians celebrate their culture and heritage.

The legacy of Christopher Columbus remains divided. He was a courageous, determined man. But he was also greedy, violent, and self-serving. What do you think? Was Christopher Columbus a hero whose ambitions opened up the New World? Or was he a villain whose greed led to the destruction of a culture?

MISTREATMENT OF THE NATIVES

"It is the poor, naked and defenseless Indians who come off the worse while the Spaniards are free to butcher them with their swords."—Bartolomé de las Casas, a Spaniard in the Americas during the time of Columbus

indigenous: native to a place

GLOSSARY

admiral (AD-muh-ruhl)—an officer with a high rank

civilization (si-vuh-ly-ZAY-shuhn)—a society that is highly developed

colonize (KAH-luh-ize)—to settle and control a territory outside of one's own country

colony (KAH-luh-nee)—territory settled by people from another country and controlled by that country

committee (kuh-MI-tee)—a group of people chosen to discuss things and make decisions for a larger group

eclipse (i-KLIPS)—an astronomical event in which the earth's shadow passes over the moon or the moon's shadow passes over the earth

gallows (GAL-ohz)—a wooden frame that holds a rope used to hang criminals

indigenous (in-DIJ-un-uhss)—native to a place

merchant (MUR-chuhnt)—relating to or used in trade

New World (NOO WURLD)—the word for what is now North and South America in the 1500s

profit (PROF-it)—money that a business makes

rebellion (ri-BEL-yuhn)—a fight against the people in charge

Revolutionary War (rev-uh-LOO-shun-ayr-ee WAR)—the American Colonies' fight for freedom from Great Britain

settlement (SET-uhl-muhnt)—a group of people living in a new village or area

Allen, Kathy. *When Did Columbus Arrive in the Americas? And Other Questions about Columbus's Voyages.* Six Questions of American History. Minneapolis: Lerner Publications, 2012.

Asselin, Kristine Carlson. *Who Really Discovered America?* Race for History. Mankato, Minn.: Capstone Press, 2011.

Feinstein, Stephen. *Columbus: Opening Up the New World.* Great Explorers of the World. Berkeley Heights, N.J.: Enslow Publishers, 2009.

INTERNET SITES

FactHound offers a safe, fun way to find Internet sites related to this book. All of the sites on FactHound have been researched by our staff.

Here's all you do:
Visit *www.facthound.com*
Type in this code: 9781476502427

Super-cool stuff! Check out projects, games and lots more at
www.capstonekids.com

CRITICAL THINKING USING THE COMMON CORE

1. Columbus was Italian, but Spain funded his expeditions. Suppose another country had paid for these trips. What might be different about North and South America? Explain your answer. (Integration of Knowledge and Ideas)

2. Upon returning to Spain for the first time, Columbus lied to the king and queen about his discoveries. Explain the effect of his actions. Use evidence from the text to support your answer. (Key Ideas and Details)

3. Read the photo caption on page 28 and examine the photograph. Think about the message the sculptor may have been trying to express as he crafted the sculpture. What do you think he wanted to say? Why do you think so? (Craft and Structure)

INDEX